coke

OR

pepsi?

The book that started it all!

What do you really know about your friends?

FINE print
PUBLISHING

2nd Edition

Written and designed by
Mickey & Cheryl Gill

Fine Print Publishing Company
P.O. Box 916401
Longwood, Florida 32791-6401

ISBN 978-189295166-3

2 4 6 8 10 9 7 5 3 1

coke-or-pepsi.com

PASS THIS BOOK AROUND TO ALL YOUR FRIENDS.

EACH ONE GETS TO ANSWER A BUNCH OF AWESOMELY
FUN QUESTIONS. COMPARE ALL YOUR ANSWERS —
SEE HOW YOU'RE DIFFERENT, SEE HOW YOU'RE
THE SAME. FIND OUT WHAT
YOUR FRIENDS ARE REALLY ALL ABOUT!

crazy bunny ...

Fave costume you've ever worn?

Ever a teacher's pet?
○ yes ○ no

○ WAFFLE CONE
○ SUGAR CONE
○ CUP

Who would you switch places with for one day?

with sprinkles

Who would you be?
○ Director ○ Actor
○ Makeup artist ○ Set designer

MY BIGGEST ? ABOUT LIFE?

WHAT ARE GNATS FOR?

1. Name? _____

2. Ever a teacher's pet? ◯ Yep ◯ No way!

3. Favorite candy? _____

4. ◯ Text ◯ IM ◯ Video-chat?

5. What makes you crazy? _____

6. Broken a body part? ◯ Nope ◯ Yep, broke my _____

7. Your biggest question about life? _____

8. Is your glass ½ ◯ full ◯ empty?

9. Most beautiful person (inside) you know? _____

10. How do you chill? _____

11. ◯ Social butterfly ◯ Wallflower?

12. Last accident/mess you caused? _____

13. Favorite relative? _____

14. Make your bed every a.m.? ◯ Yes ◯ No

15. Names of future children? _____

MY FAVE COLOR OF EYES R RAINBOW

16. ○ Secret keeper ○ Blabbermouth?

17. Favorite color of eyes? _____

18. ○ Klutzy ○ Sure-footed?

19. Latest wish? _____

20. Been sent to the principal's office? ○ Yep ○ Nope

21. ○ Morning glory ○ Night owl?

22. Favorite forest animal? _____

23. Birthmark? ○ Yes ○ No

24. Dream job? _____

25. ○ Store-bought ○ Homemade?

26. Something you don't understand? _____

27. Who would you be? ○ Director ○ Actor ○ Makeup artist ○ Set designer

28. What do u nosh on & drink at the movies? _____

29. What makes you cry? _____

30. Coolest color for a car? _____

coke or pepsi?

{ What is your full name? } Nickname?

coke OR pepsi?

Favorite song?

Earliest memory?

Who do you call when you're upset?

○ **TV**
○ **Book?**

Last book you read?

○ **Milk** ○ **Dark** chocolate?

● Clean freak
● Total slob?

What kind of shoes are you wearing?

Fave store?

○ **Beach**
○ **Mountains?**

Do you recycle?
○ yes
○ no

Do you wish on
○ yes
○ no

○ **Big Mac**
○ **Whopper?**

Shirt
● tucked ● out?

Best gift you've ever received?

Best gift you've ever given?

Coolest car?

Ever been stung by a jellyfish? ○ yes ○ no

Stupidest thing you've ever done ?

Best sitcom ever?

○ Dreamer
○ Doer?

Favorite doughnut?
_ _ _ _ _

1 word 2 describe U?

Best cartoon ever? _

Last person you spoke to? _

Least favorite vegetable? _

Name of your very first friend? _ _ _ _ _ _ _ _ _ _ _ _ _ _ _ _ _

If u could, what would you change your name to? _ _ _ _ _ _ _ _ _ _

Favorite place you've visited? _ _ _ _ _ _ _ _ _ _ _ _ _ _ _ _ _ _ _

Ever pull an all-nighter?
○ yes ○ no

Believe in love at first sight?
○ yes ○ no

Been to **NYC?**
○ yes
○ no

Best pizza toppings? _ _ _ _ _ _ _ _

_ _ _ _ _ _ _ _ _ _ _ _

● Night light
● Completely dark?

scares you?

What

_ _ _ _ _

_ _ _ _ _

Been to **L.A.?**
○ yes ○ no

hamburger?

Gotta have double cheese

1. What are your initials? _____

2. ○ Ice cubes   ○ Crushed ice?

3. What do you like on your burger? _____

4. Who do you admire the most? _____

5. How do your parents dance?   ○ Awesomely   ○ Terribly

6. Favorite food court place? _____

7. Worst appointment ever?   ○ Doctor   ○ Dentist

8. How old were you when you learned to swim? _____

9. ○ Bagel   ○ Doughnut   ○ Croissant   ○ Cinnamon roll?

10. Favorite department store? _____

11. Know sign language?   ○ Yes   ○ No

12. Who taught you to ride a bike? _____

13. Been to the emergency room?   ○ Yes   ○ No

14. Last dream you remember? _____

15. Word or phrase you say a lot? _____

Fave cookie is

16. Worry ○ wart ○ free?

17. Worst movie ever? _____

18. ○ Reality show ○ Sitcom?

19. Best commercial? _____

20. Yummiest smoothie? _____

21. Fave brand of jeans? _____

22. Who would u be in the castle? ○ Queen ○ Princess ○ Knight ○ Jester

23. Game you liked as a kid? _____

24. Like to eat ○ a lot of different things ○ mainly fruits & veggies?

25. Advice for a 5-year-old? _____

26. Best type of movie? ○ Romance ○ Comedy ○ Scary ○ Action ○ Sci-Fi

27. Favorite author? _____

28. Most awesome cookie? _____

29. Tastiest fast food? _____

30. Time ○ drags ○ goes by too fast?

1. First, middle, and last name? _____

2. Believe in UFOs? ◯ Yes! ◯ No!

3. What can't you live without? _____

4. Can you identify constellations? ◯ Yes ◯ No

5. Meanest thing you've done to a sibling?_____

6. ◯ Creamy   ◯ Crunchy peanut butter?

7. Take vitamins? ◯ Yeah ◯ Nah

8. Awesome little kid movie?_____

9. Someone or something you miss?_____

10. Floss? ◯ Yeah ◯ Nah

11. Believe in the Loch Ness monster? ◯ Yeah ◯ Nah

12. ◯ Apple ◯ Orange ◯ Pear ◯ Other _____ ?

13. WWYRH?* ◯ $50/week ◯ 3-day weekend

14. Any pets? ◯ No ◯ Yes, _____
kinds

15. If yes to #14, names? _____

* *Slang key* WWYRH = What would you rather have

16. Best amusement park ride? _____

17. ◯ Train ◯ Plane ◯ Automobile?

18. How would you change your hair? _____

19. Museum of ◯ art ◯ natural history?

20. Believe in Bigfoot? ◯ Of course ◯ No way

21. Up to date on current news? ◯ Yes ◯ No

22. What's not fair? _____

23. ◯ Waffle cone ◯ Sugar cone ◯ Cup?

24. Favorite costume you've ever worn? _____

25. Which is worse? No ◯ TV ◯ Music

26. Best fairy tale? _____

27. ◯ Small purse ◯ Giant bag?

28. Ever have an imaginary friend? ◯ No ◯ Yes, _____

29. Can different foods touch on your plate? ◯ Yes ◯ No

30. Favorite pair of shoes? _____

coke or pepsi?

{ Name given at birth?

○ **Coffee**
○ **Tea?**

What do your friends call you?

Favorite holiday and why? ✔

What do you do when you're mad?

Favorite actor?

○ Radio ○ iPod
○ Other?

Favorite actress?

Ever won anything?
○ yes ○ no
↓ What?

Flower u love?

Oldest living relative?

Most annoying bug?

Best kind of music?

○ 🐕 ○ 🐈
person?

What do you do on rainy days?

Ever been in love?
○ yes ○ no

Nails:
○ Painted
○ Chipped
○ Fake
○ Bitten?

Wear painful shoes just because they're cute?
○ yes
○ no

○ **Tanning oil**
○ **Sunscreen?**

Have a secret you've never told?
○ yes ○ no

Fave thing to nosh on? _ _ _ _ _ _ _ _ _ _ _ _ _ _ _ _ _ _

Did you ever believe in the Tooth Fairy?
○ yes ○ nah

Your absolute favorite article of clothing?

○ Spender ○ Saver?

What superpower would you love to have?

Cosmetic you can't live without?

Would you try?
○ Skydiving
○ Rappelling
○ Scuba Diving

○ Butterflies
○ Dragonflies?

○ Organic
○ Junk food?

Who do you wish you could meet? 👉

Best beverage?

Cereal you love?

Who should play you in a movie version of your life?
_ _

If you were an animal what would you be?
_ _

Best teacher you've ever had? _ _ _ _ _ _ _ _

Favorite school subject? _ _ _ _ _ _ _ _ _ _

● Fro yo ● Ice cream?

● Mall ● Outlet?

● Chips ● Fries?

● Fearless ● Fearful?

BEST FRIEND
SINCE KINDERGARTEN

1. Name? _____

2. Where were you born? _____

3. Favorite picture book? _____

4. ⚪ Hot dog   ⚪ Hamburger?

5. Invention you would love? _____

6. Friend you've had the longest? _____

7. ⚪ White   ⚪ Wheat?

8. Best fashion era?   ⚪ 60s ⚪ 70s ⚪ 80s ⚪ 90s ⚪ Now

9. How many hours per day online? _____

10. How many hours per day texting? _____

11. What's scarier? ⚪ Snake ⚪ Shark

12. What do you always say "no" to? _____

13. Favorite food comes from which country? _____

14. Try to run away from home when you were little? ⚪ Yes ⚪ No

15. What are you not good at? _____

FARAWAY FRIEND

SO MANY MILES ...

16. Something you would like to try? _____

17. ◯ Chocolate ◯ Soy ◯ Almond milk?

18. Friend who lives the farthest from you? _____

19. Where does #18 friend live? _____

20. Which could you give up? ◯ Email ◯ Cell phone

21. ◯ Flip-flops ◯ Strappy sandals?

22. Favorite season? _____ Why? _____

23. Read the ending before finishing a book? ◯ Yes ◯ No

24. Who would you switch places with for one day? _____

25. ◯ Island cabana ◯ European castle ◯ Safari tent ◯ Ski lodge?

26. What scared you as a little kid? _____

27. Favorite number? _____ Why? _____

28. ◯ Right-handed ◯ Left-handed ◯ Ambidextrous?

29. Color your toes are painted? _____

30. Ever needed stitches? ◯ No ◯ Yes, for _____

1. Name? _____

2. Birthday? _____

3. Something you can't stand the smell of? _____

4. Look for shapes in the clouds? ◯ Yes ◯ No

5. Coolest thing you learned this week? _____

6. What are you good at? _____

7. ◯ Great vision ◯ Glasses ◯ Contacts?

8. Favorite take-out food? _____

9. Something you can't wait to do? _____

10. ◯ Salty ◯ Sweet?

11. Swallow anything by accident as a kid? ◯ No ◯ Yes, _____

12. Favorite accessory? _____

13. ◯ Lone Ranger ◯ Team Player?

14. ◯ Bikini ◯ One-piece?

15. Ever been snowed in? ◯ No ◯ Yes

16. Take pictures with ◯ camera ◯ phone?

17. Something you like to listen to? _____

18. ◯ Tap ◯ Bottled ◯ Sparkling water?

19. What was your fave thing on the playground? _____

20. What would you love to see? _____

21. Favorite hot beverage? _____

22. Habit you wish you could change?_____

23. Are you a sore loser? ◯ Yes ◯ No

24. Yummiest ice cream flavor? _____

25. ◯ Pilot ◯ Navigator?

26. Who influences you the most? _____

27. Have you ever re-gifted? ◯ No ◯ Yes, _____

28. ◯ Toilet-papered ◯ Toilet-paperer?

29. What do you daydream about? _____

30. ◯ Small talk ◯ Deep conversation?

Travel back to the building of the pyramids

1. Nickname? _____

2. Shop ◯ alone   ◯ with mom   ◯ with friends?

3. ◯ Kill bugs   ◯ Try to save them?

4. Favorite scent? _____

5. ◯ Manicure   ◯ DIY nails?

6. Been in a talent show? ◯ No ◯ Yes, I _____

7. What's your current fave song about? _____

8. How do you like your popcorn? _____

9. ◯ Mild   ◯ Medium   ◯ Spicy?

10. Magazine you love? _____

11. ◯ Details   ◯ Big picture?

12. Favorite comfort food? _____

13. ◯ Super trendy   ◯ Totally casual?

14. Best friend in kindergarten? _____

15. What can't you bear the sound of? _____

TRAVEL FORWARD TO SEE IF I LIVE ON A MOON BASE

16. ◯ Gold   ◯ Silver   ◯ Costume jewelry?

17. Coolest first name? _____

18. Favorite hangout? _____

19. Ever think there was a monster under your bed? ◯ Yes ◯ No

20. ◯ Brownies   ◯ Chocolate chip cookies?

21. Favorite thing to do on the weekend? _____

22. Where & when would you like to time-travel back to? _____

23. Where & when would you like to time-travel forward to? _____

24. What can you draw well? _____

25. ◯ Go with the flow   ◯ Stick to a routine?

26. Best type of cake? _____

27. ◯ Polka dots   ◯ Stripes   ◯ Plaid   ◯ Paisley?

28. What do you do after school? _____

29. ◯ Hang with friends   ◯ Go to a party?

30. How many times have you moved in your life? _____

What do I like to shop for?

super fun earrings!

1. Name? _____

2. How tall are you? _____

3. Camping in a ◯ cabin ◯ tent?

4. Kind of toothpaste you use? _____

5. What color is your bedroom? _____

6. Something that makes you nervous? _____

7. Make your bed every a.m.? ◯ Yes ◯ No

8. What did you do last night? _____

9. Biscuits with ◯ honey ◯ jam?

10. Awesome color combo? _____

11. Worse shopping for ◯ jeans ◯ bikini?

12. Number of children you would like someday? _____

13. ◯ Sunrise ◯ Sunset?

14. Coolest last name? _____

15. As a little kid, ◯ stuffed animal ◯ blankie?

16. ◯ Shower ◯ Bath?

17. Ever owned a goldfish? ◯ No ◯ Yes, _____
name

18. Cutest thing your pet does? _____

19. Something you refuse to eat? _____

20. Kind of bubblegum bubble blower are you? ◯ OK ◯ Highly skilled ◯ Awful

21. Fave pizza place? _____

22. What would be hard to give up? _____

23. Last thing you ate? _____

24. Push elevator buttons more than once? ◯ Never ◯ Always

25. Newest friend? _____

26. Love to see a ◯ volcano eruption ◯ solar eclipse?

27. Something you like to shop for? _____

28. What would you ask your future self? _____

29. ◯ Rollerblade ◯ Ice skate ◯ Skateboard ◯ None?

30. Afraid of spiders? ◯ YES! ◯ Nah

MY BIGGEST ? ABOUT LIFE?

WHAT ARE GNATS FOR?

1. Name? _____

2. Ever a teacher's pet? ○ Yep ○ No way!

3. Favorite candy? _____

4. ○ Text ○ IM ○ Video-chat?

5. What makes you crazy? _____

6. Broken a body part? ○ Nope ○ Yep, broke my _____

7. Your biggest question about life? _____

8. Is your glass ½ ○ full ○ empty?

9. Most beautiful person (inside) you know? _____

10. How do you chill? _____

11. ○ Social butterfly ○ Wallflower?

12. Last accident/mess you caused? _____

13. Favorite relative? _____

14. Make your bed every a.m.? ○ Yes ○ No

15. Names of future children? _____

16. ◯ Secret keeper ◯ Blabbermouth?

17. Favorite color of eyes? _____

18. ◯ Klutzy ◯ Sure-footed?

19. Latest wish? _____

20. Been sent to the principal's office? ◯ Yep ◯ Nope

21. ◯ Morning glory ◯ Night owl?

22. Favorite forest animal? _____

23. Birthmark? ◯ Yes ◯ No

24. Dream job? _____

25. ◯ Store-bought ◯ Homemade?

26. Something you don't understand? _____

27. Who would you be? ◯ Director ◯ Actor ◯ Makeup artist ◯ Set designer

28. What do u nosh on & drink at the movies? _____

29. What makes you cry? _____

30. Coolest color for a car? _____

coke or pepsi?

{ What is your full name? _____ Nickname? }

coke OR **pepsi?**

Favorite song?
_____

🧠 Earliest memory? _____

Who do you call when you're upset? ▷ _____

○ **TV**
○ **Bo ok?**

Last book you read?
_____

○ **Milk** ○ **Dark chocolate?**

● Clean freak
● Total slob?

What kind of shoes are you wearing?
_____

Fave store?
_____

○ **Beach**
○ **Moun tains?**

Do you recycle?
○ yes
○ no

Do you wish on

○ **Big Mac**
○ **Whopper?**

○ yes
○ no

Coolest car?
_____

Shirt
● tucked ● out?

Best gift you've ever received?
_____

Best gift you've ever given?
_____

Ever been stung by a jellyfish? ○ yes ○ no

Stupidest thing you've ever done ?

Best sitcom ever?

○ Dreamer
○ Doer?

Favorite doughnut?
_ _ _ _ _

1 word 2 describe U? ☞

Best cartoon ever? _

Last person you spoke to? _

Least favorite vegetable? _

Name of your very first friend? _ _ _ _ _ _ _ _ _ _ _ _ _ _ _ _ _ _

If u could, what would you change your name to? _ _ _ _ _ _ _ _ _ _

Favorite place you've visited? _ _ _ _ _ _ _ _ _ _ _ _ _ _ _ _ _ _ _

Ever pull an all-nighter?
○ yes ○ no

Believe in love at first sight?
○ yes ○ no

Been to NYC?
○ yes
○ no

Best pizza toppings? _ _ _ _ _ _ _ _ _ _ _ _ _ _ _
_ _ _ _ _ _ _ _ _ _ _ _ _ _ _

Been to L.A.?
○ yes ○ no

○ Night light
○ Completely dark?

scares you?

What

hamburger? ←

Gotta have double cheese

1. What are your initials? _____

2. ◯ Ice cubes   ◯ Crushed ice?

3. What do you like on your burger? _____

4. Who do you admire the most? _____

5. How do your parents dance?   ◯ Awesomely   ◯ Terribly

6. Favorite food court place? _____

7. Worst appointment ever?   ◯ Doctor   ◯ Dentist

8. How old were you when you learned to swim? _____

9. ◯ Bagel   ◯ Doughnut   ◯ Croissant   ◯ Cinnamon roll?

10. Favorite department store? _____

11. Know sign language?   ◯ Yes   ◯ No

12. Who taught you to ride a bike? _____

13. Been to the emergency room?   ◯ Yes   ◯ No

14. Last dream you remember? _____

15. Word or phrase you say a lot? _____

chocolate chip
Fave cookie is

OH BOY!

16. Worry ○ wart ○ free?

17. Worst movie ever? _____

18. ○ Reality show ○ Sitcom?

19. Best commercial? _____

20. Yummiest smoothie? _____

21. Fave brand of jeans? _____

22. Who would u be in the castle? ○ Queen ○ Princess ○ Knight ○ Jester

23. Game you liked as a kid? _____

24. Like to eat ○ a lot of different things ○ mainly fruits & veggies?

25. Advice for a 5-year-old? _____

26. Best type of movie? ○ Romance ○ Comedy ○ Scary ○ Action ○ Sci-Fi

27. Favorite author? _____

28. Most awesome cookie? _____

29. Tastiest fast food? _____

30. Time ○ drags ○ goes by too fast?

UFO♥s? **starg**

1. First, middle, and last name? _____

2. Believe in UFOs? ○ Yes! ○ No!

3. What can't you live without? _____

4. Can you identify constellations? ○ Yes ○ No

5. Meanest thing you've done to a sibling? _____

6. ○ Creamy ○ Crunchy peanut butter?

7. Take vitamins? ○ Yeah ○ Nah

8. Awesome little kid movie? _____

9. Someone or something you miss? _____

10. Floss? ○ Yeah ○ Nah

11. Believe in the Loch Ness monster? ○ Yeah ○ Nah

12. ○ Apple ○ Orange ○ Pear ○ Other _____ ?

13. WWYRH?* ○ $50/week ○ 3-day weekend

14. Any pets? ○ No ○ Yes, _____
kinds

15. If yes to #14, names? _____

* *Slang key* WWYRH = What would you rather have

Yes way!
oh, please

16. Best amusement park ride? _____

17. ◯ Train ◯ Plane ◯ Automobile?

18. How would you change your hair? _____

19. Museum of ◯ art ◯ natural history?

20. Believe in Bigfoot? ◯ Of course ◯ No way

21. Up to date on current news? ◯ Yes ◯ No

22. What's not fair? _____

23. ◯ Waffle cone ◯ Sugar cone ◯ Cup?

24. Favorite costume you've ever worn? _____

25. Which is worse? No ◯ TV ◯ Music

26. Best fairy tale? _____

27. ◯ Small purse ◯ Giant bag?

28. Ever have an imaginary friend? ◯ No ◯ Yes, _____

29. Can different foods touch on your plate? ◯ Yes ◯ No

30. Favorite pair of shoes? _____

coke or pepsi?

{ Name given at birth?

○ **Coffee**
○ **Tea?**

What do your friends call you? ▶

Favorite holiday and why? ✔

What do you do when you're mad?

○ Radio ○ iPod
○ Other?

Favorite actor?

Favorite actress?

Ever won anything?
○ yes ○ no
↓ What?

Flower u love?

Oldest living relative?

Most annoying bug?

Best kind of music?

○ ○
person?

What do you do on rainy days?

Ever been in love?
○ yes ○ no

○ **Tanning oil**
○ **Sunscreen?**

Nails:
○ Painted
○ Chipped
○ Fake
○ Bitten?

Wear painful shoes just because they're cute?
○ yes
○ no

Have a secret you've never told?
○ yes ○ no

Fave thing to nosh on?

Did you ever believe in the Tooth Fairy? ○ yes ○ nah

Your absolute favorite article of clothing?

○ Spender ○ Saver?

Fro yo ○ **Ice cream?**

What superpower would you love to have?

Cosmetic you can't live without?

Would you try?
○ Skydiving
○ Rappelling
○ Scuba Diving

○ Butterflies
○ Dragonflies?

○ Organic
○ Junk food?

Mall ○ **Outlet?**

Who do you wish you could meet? ☞

Best beverage?

Chips ○ **Fries?**

Cereal you love?

Who should play you in a movie version of your life?

If you were an animal what would you be?

Fearless ○ **Fearful?**

Best teacher you've ever had?

Favorite school subject?

BEST FRIEND

SINCE KINDERGARTEN

1. Name? _____

2. Where were you born? _____

3. Favorite picture book? _____

4. ◯ Hot dog ◯ Hamburger?

5. Invention you would love? _____

6. Friend you've had the longest? _____

7. ◯ White ◯ Wheat?

8. Best fashion era? ◯ 60s ◯ 70s ◯ 80s ◯ 90s ◯ Now

9. How many hours per day online? _____

10. How many hours per day texting? _____

11. What's scarier? ◯ Snake ◯ Shark

12. What do you always say "no" to? _____

13. Favorite food comes from which country? _____

14. Try to run away from home when you were little? ◯ Yes ◯ No

15. What are you not good at? _____

16. Something you would like to try? _____

17. ○ Chocolate   ○ Soy   ○ Almond milk?

18. Friend who lives the farthest from you? _____

19. Where does #18 friend live? _____

20. Which could you give up? ○ Email   ○ Cell phone

21. ○ Flip-flops   ○ Strappy sandals?

22. Favorite season? _____ Why? _____

23. Read the ending before finishing a book? ○ Yes   ○ No

24. Who would you switch places with for one day? _____

25. ○ Island cabana   ○ European castle   ○ Safari tent   ○ Ski lodge?

26. What scared you as a little kid? _____

27. Favorite number? _____ Why? _____

28. ○ Right-handed   ○ Left-handed   ○ Ambidextrous?

29. Color your toes are painted? _____

30. Ever needed stitches? ○ No   ○ Yes, for _____

I always find animals in the clouds

1. Name? _____

2. Birthday? _____

3. Something you can't stand the smell of? _____

4. Look for shapes in the clouds? ○ Yes ○ No

5. Coolest thing you learned this week? _____

6. What are you good at? _____

7. ○ Great vision ○ Glasses ○ Contacts?

8. Favorite take-out food? _____

9. Something you can't wait to do? _____

10. ○ Salty ○ Sweet?

11. Swallow anything by accident as a kid? ○ No ○ Yes, _____

12. Favorite accessory? _____

13. ○ Lone Ranger ○ Team Player?

14. ○ Bikini ○ One-piece?

15. Ever been snowed in? ○ No ○ Yes

I dream of flying to exotic lands

16. Take pictures with ○ camera ○ phone?

17. Something you like to listen to? _____

18. ○ Tap ○ Bottled ○ Sparkling water?

19. What was your fave thing on the playground? _____

20. What would you love to see? _____

21. Favorite hot beverage? _____

22. Habit you wish you could change? _____

23. Are you a sore loser? ○ Yes ○ No

24. Yummiest ice cream flavor? _____

25. ○ Pilot ○ Navigator?

26. Who influences you the most? _____

27. Have you ever re-gifted? ○ No ○ Yes, _____

28. ○ Toilet-papered ○ Toilet-paperer?

29. What do you daydream about? _____

30. ○ Small talk ○ Deep conversation?

Travel back to the building of the pyramids

1. Nickname? _____

2. Shop ◯ alone ◯ with mom ◯ with friends?

3. ◯ Kill bugs ◯ Try to save them?

4. Favorite scent? _____

5. ◯ Manicure ◯ DIY nails?

6. Been in a talent show? ◯ No ◯ Yes, I _____

7. What's your current fave song about? _____

8. How do you like your popcorn? _____

9. ◯ Mild ◯ Medium ◯ Spicy?

10. Magazine you love? _____

11. ◯ Details ◯ Big picture?

12. Favorite comfort food? _____

13. ◯ Super trendy ◯ Totally casual?

14. Best friend in kindergarten? _____

15. What can't you bear the sound of? _____

TRAVEL FORWARD TO SEE IF I LIVE ON A MOON BASE

16. ◯ Gold   ◯ Silver   ◯ Costume jewelry?

17. Coolest first name? _____

18. Favorite hangout? _____

19. Ever think there was a monster under your bed? ◯ Yes ◯ No

20. ◯ Brownies   ◯ Chocolate chip cookies?

21. Favorite thing to do on the weekend? _____

22. Where & when would you like to time-travel back to? _____

23. Where & when would you like to time-travel forward to? _____

24. What can you draw well? _____

25. ◯ Go with the flow   ◯ Stick to a routine?

26. Best type of cake? _____

27. ◯ Polka dots   ◯ Stripes   ◯ Plaid   ◯ Paisley?

28. What do you do after school? _____

29. ◯ Hang with friends   ◯ Go to a party?

30. How many times have you moved in your life? _____

What do I like to shop for?

super fun earrings!

1. Name? _____

2. How tall are you? _____

3. Camping in a ◯ cabin ◯ tent?

4. Kind of toothpaste you use? _____

5. What color is your bedroom? _____

6. Something that makes you nervous? _____

7. Make your bed every a.m.? ◯ Yes ◯ No

8. What did you do last night? _____

9. Biscuits with ◯ honey ◯ jam?

10. Awesome color combo? _____

11. Worse shopping for ◯ jeans ◯ bikini?

12. Number of children you would like someday? _____

13. ◯ Sunrise ◯ Sunset?

14. Coolest last name? _____

15. As a little kid, ◯ stuffed animal ◯ blankie?

16. ◯ Shower ◯ Bath?

17. Ever owned a goldfish? ◯ No ◯ Yes, _____
name

18. Cutest thing your pet does? _____

19. Something you refuse to eat? _____

20. Kind of bubblegum bubble blower are you? ◯ OK ◯ Highly skilled ◯ Awful

21. Fave pizza place? _____

22. What would be hard to give up?_____

23. Last thing you ate? _____

24. Push elevator buttons more than once? ◯ Never ◯ Always

25. Newest friend? _____

26. Love to see a ◯ volcano eruption ◯ solar eclipse?

27. Something you like to shop for?_____

28. What would you ask your future self? _____

29. ◯ Rollerblade ◯ Ice skate ◯ Skateboard ◯ None?

30. Afraid of spiders? ◯ YES! ◯ Nah

1. Name? _____

2. Ever a teacher's pet? ◯ Yep ◯ No way!

3. Favorite candy? _____

4. ◯ Text ◯ IM ◯ Video-chat?

5. What makes you crazy? _____

6. Broken a body part? ◯ Nope ◯ Yep, broke my _____

7. Your biggest question about life? _____

8. Is your glass ½ ◯ full ◯ empty?

9. Most beautiful person (inside) you know? _____

10. How do you chill? _____

11. ◯ Social butterfly ◯ Wallflower?

12. Last accident/mess you caused? _____

13. Favorite relative? _____

14. Make your bed every a.m.? ◯ Yes ◯ No

15. Names of future children? _____

16. ◯ Secret keeper ◯ Blabbermouth?

17. Favorite color of eyes? _____

18. ◯ Klutzy ◯ Sure-footed?

19. Latest wish? _____

20. Been sent to the principal's office? ◯ Yep ◯ Nope

21. ◯ Morning glory ◯ Night owl?

22. Favorite forest animal? _____

23. Birthmark? ◯ Yes ◯ No

24. Dream job? _____

25. ◯ Store-bought ◯ Homemade?

26. Something you don't understand? _____

27. Who would you be? ◯ Director ◯ Actor ◯ Makeup artist ◯ Set designer

28. What do u nosh on & drink at the movies? _____

29. What makes you cry? _____

30. Coolest color for a car? _____

coke or pepsi?

{ What is your full name? }

Nickname?

coke OR **pepsi?**

Favorite song?

Earliest memory?

Who do you call when you're upset?

○ **TV**
○ **Book?**

Last book you read?

○ **Milk** ○ **Dark chocolate?**

● Clean freak
● Total slob?

What kind of shoes are you wearing?

Fave store?

○ **Beach**
○ **Mountains?**

Do you recycle?
○ yes
○ no

Do you wish on

○ **Big Mac**
○ **Whopper?**

○ yes
○ no

Shirt
● tucked ● out?

Best gift you've ever received?

Best gift you've ever given?

Coolest car?

Ever been stung by a jellyfish? ○ yes ○ no

Stupidest thing you've ever done ▼

Best sitcom ever?

○ Dreamer
○ Doer?

Favorite doughnut?
_ _ _ _

1 word 2 ☞
describe U?

Best cartoon ever? _ _ _ _ _ _ _ _ _ _ _ _

Last person you spoke to? _ _ _ _ _ _ _ _ _ _ _ _

Least favorite vegetable? _ _ _ _ _ _ _ _ _ _ _ _

Name of your very first friend? _ _ _ _ _ _ _ _ _ _

If u could, what would you change your name to? _ _ _ _ _ _ _ _ _

Favorite place you've visited? _ _ _ _ _ _ _ _ _ _

Ever pull an all-nighter?
○ yes ○ no

Believe in love at first sight?
○ yes ○ no

Been to NYC?
○ yes
○ no

Best pizza toppings? _ _ _ _ _ _ _
_ _ _ _ _ _ _

● Night light
● Completely dark?

scares you?

What

Been to L.A.?
○ yes ○ no

hamburger?
Gotta have double cheese

1. What are your initials? _____

2. ◯ Ice cubes   ◯ Crushed ice?

3. What do you like on your burger? _____

4. Who do you admire the most? _____

5. How do your parents dance? ◯ Awesomely ◯ Terribly

6. Favorite food court place? _____

7. Worst appointment ever? ◯ Doctor ◯ Dentist

8. How old were you when you learned to swim? _____

9. ◯ Bagel   ◯ Doughnut   ◯ Croissant   ◯ Cinnamon roll?

10. Favorite department store? _____

11. Know sign language? ◯ Yes ◯ No

12. Who taught you to ride a bike? _____

13. Been to the emergency room? ◯ Yes ◯ No

14. Last dream you remember? _____

15. Word or phrase you say a lot? _____

OH BOY!

16. Worry ○ wart ○ free?

17. Worst movie ever? _____

18. ○ Reality show ○ Sitcom?

19. Best commercial? _____

20. Yummiest smoothie? _____

21. Fave brand of jeans? _____

22. Who would u be in the castle? ○ Queen ○ Princess ○ Knight ○ Jester

23. Game you liked as a kid? _____

24. Like to eat ○ a lot of different things ○ mainly fruits & veggies?

25. Advice for a 5-year-old? _____

26. Best type of movie? ○ Romance ○ Comedy ○ Scary ○ Action ○ Sci-Fi

27. Favorite author? _____

28. Most awesome cookie? _____

29. Tastiest fast food? _____

30. Time ○ drags ○ goes by too fast?

UFO♡s? star...

1. First, middle, and last name? _____

2. Believe in UFOs? ◯ Yes! ◯ No!

3. What can't you live without? _____

4. Can you identify constellations? ◯ Yes ◯ No

5. Meanest thing you've done to a sibling?_____

6. ◯ Creamy ◯ Crunchy peanut butter?

7. Take vitamins? ◯ Yeah ◯ Nah

8. Awesome little kid movie?_____

9. Someone or something you miss? _____

10. Floss? ◯ Yeah ◯ Nah

11. Believe in the Loch Ness monster? ◯ Yeah ◯ Nah

12. ◯ Apple ◯ Orange ◯ Pear ◯ Other _____?

13. WWYRH?* ◯ $50/week ◯ 3-day weekend

14. Any pets? ◯ No ◯ Yes, _____
   kinds

15. If yes to #14, names? _____

* *Slang key* WWYRH = What would you rather have

16. Best amusement park ride? _____

17. ◯ Train ◯ Plane ◯ Automobile?

18. How would you change your hair? _____

19. Museum of ◯ art ◯ natural history?

20. Believe in Bigfoot? ◯ Of course ◯ No way

21. Up to date on current news? ◯ Yes ◯ No

22. What's not fair? _____

23. ◯ Waffle cone ◯ Sugar cone ◯ Cup?

24. Favorite costume you've ever worn? _____

25. Which is worse? No ◯ TV ◯ Music

26. Best fairy tale? _____

27. ◯ Small purse ◯ Giant bag?

28. Ever have an imaginary friend? ◯ No ◯ Yes, _____

29. Can different foods touch on your plate? ◯ Yes ◯ No

30. Favorite pair of shoes? _____

coke or pepsi?

{ Name given at birth?

○ **Coffee**
○ **Tea?**

What do your friends call you?

Favorite holiday and why? ✔

What do you do when you're mad?

Favorite actor?

○ Radio ○ iPod
○ Other? _ _ _ _ _ _

Favorite actress?

Ever won anything?
○ yes ○ no
↓ What?

Flower u love? _ _ _ _ _ _ _ _ _ _ _

Oldest living relative? _ _ _ _ _ _ _

Most annoying bug? _ _ _ _ _ _ _ _

Best kind of music? _ _ _ _ _ _ _ _

○ 🐕 ○ 🐈
person?

Ever been in love?
○ yes ○ no

What do you do on rainy days?

Nails:
○ Painted
○ Chipped
○ Fake
○ Bitten?

Wear painful shoes just because they're cute?
○ yes
○ no

○ **Tanning oil**
○ **Sunscreen?**

Have a secret you've never told?
○ yes ○ no

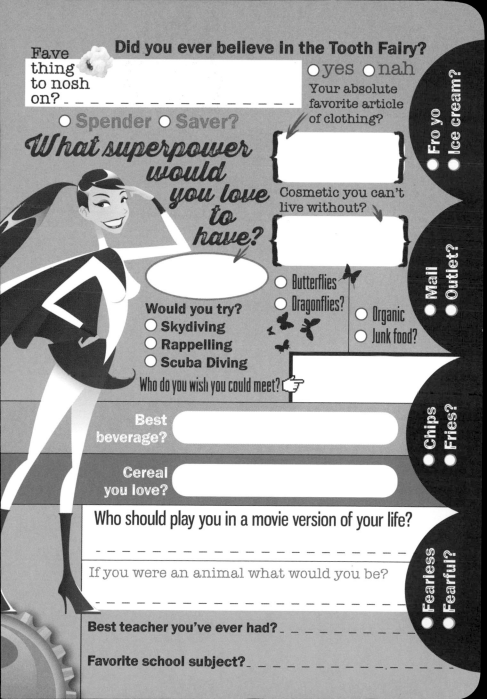

Fave thing to nosh on? _ _ _ _ _ _ _ _ _ _ _ _ _

Did you ever believe in the Tooth Fairy?

○ yes ○ nah

Your absolute favorite article of clothing?

○ Spender ○ Saver?

What superpower would you love to have?

Cosmetic you can't live without?

○ Butterflies
○ Dragonflies?

Would you try?
○ **Skydiving**
○ **Rappelling**
○ **Scuba Diving**

○ Organic
○ Junk food?

Who do you wish you could meet? ☞

Best beverage?

Cereal you love?

Who should play you in a movie version of your life?
_ _ _ _ _ _ _ _ _ _ _ _ _

If you were an animal what would you be?
_ _ _ _ _ _ _ _ _ _ _ _ _

Best teacher you've ever had? _ _ _ _ _ _ _

Favorite school subject? _ _ _ _ _ _ _

● Fro yo
● Ice cream?

● Mall
● Outlet?

● Chips
● Fries?

● Fearless
● Fearful?

BEST FRIEND

SINCE KINDERGARTEN

1. Name? _____

2. Where were you born? _____

3. Favorite picture book? _____

4. ◯ Hot dog   ◯ Hamburger?

5. Invention you would love? _____

6. Friend you've had the longest? _____

7. ◯ White   ◯ Wheat?

8. Best fashion era?   ◯ 60s ◯ 70s ◯ 80s ◯ 90s ◯ Now

9. How many hours per day online? _____

10. How many hours per day texting? _____

11. What's scarier?   ◯ Snake   ◯ Shark

12. What do you always say "no" to? _____

13. Favorite food comes from which country? _____

14. Try to run away from home when you were little?   ◯ Yes ◯ No

15. What are you not good at? _____

16. Something you would like to try? _____

17. ⦿ Chocolate ⦿ Soy ⦿ Almond milk?

18. Friend who lives the farthest from you? _____

19. Where does #18 friend live? _____

20. Which could you give up? ⦿ Email ⦿ Cell phone

21. ⦿ Flip-flops ⦿ Strappy sandals?

22. Favorite season? _____ Why? _____

23. Read the ending before finishing a book? ⦿ Yes ⦿ No

24. Who would you switch places with for one day? _____

25. ⦿ Island cabana ⦿ European castle ⦿ Safari tent ⦿ Ski lodge?

26. What scared you as a little kid? _____

27. Favorite number? _____ Why? _____

28. ⦿ Right-handed ⦿ Left-handed ⦿ Ambidextrous?

29. Color your toes are painted? _____

30. Ever needed stitches? ⦿ No ⦿ Yes, for _____

I always find animals in the clouds

1. Name? _____

2. Birthday? _____

3. Something you can't stand the smell of? _____

4. Look for shapes in the clouds? ○ Yes ○ No

5. Coolest thing you learned this week? _____

6. What are you good at? _____

7. ○ Great vision ○ Glasses ○ Contacts?

8. Favorite take-out food? _____

9. Something you can't wait to do? _____

10. ○ Salty ○ Sweet?

11. Swallow anything by accident as a kid? ○ No ○ Yes, _____

12. Favorite accessory? _____

13. ○ Lone Ranger ○ Team Player?

14. ○ Bikini ○ One-piece?

15. Ever been snowed in? ○ No ○ Yes

16. Take pictures with ◯ camera ◯ phone?

17. Something you like to listen to? _____

18. ◯ Tap ◯ Bottled ◯ Sparkling water?

19. What was your fave thing on the playground? _____

20. What would you love to see? _____

21. Favorite hot beverage? _____

22. Habit you wish you could change? _____

23. Are you a sore loser? ◯ Yes ◯ No

24. Yummiest ice cream flavor? _____

25. ◯ Pilot ◯ Navigator?

26. Who influences you the most? _____

27. Have you ever re-gifted? ◯ No ◯ Yes, _____

28. ◯ Toilet-papered ◯ Toilet-paperer?

29. What do you daydream about? _____

30. ◯ Small talk ◯ Deep conversation?

Travel back to the building of the pyramids

1. Nickname? _____

2. Shop ◯ alone ◯ with mom ◯ with friends?

3. ◯ Kill bugs ◯ Try to save them?

4. Favorite scent? _____

5. ◯ Manicure ◯ DIY nails?

6. Been in a talent show? ◯ No ◯ Yes, I _____

7. What's your current fave song about? _____

8. How do you like your popcorn? _____

9. ◯ Mild ◯ Medium ◯ Spicy?

10. Magazine you love? _____

11. ◯ Details ◯ Big picture?

12. Favorite comfort food? _____

13. ◯ Super trendy ◯ Totally casual?

14. Best friend in kindergarten? _____

15. What can't you bear the sound of? _____

16. ◯ Gold   ◯ Silver   ◯ Costume jewelry?

17. Coolest first name? _____

18. Favorite hangout? _____

19. Ever think there was a monster under your bed? ◯ Yes ◯ No

20. ◯ Brownies   ◯ Chocolate chip cookies?

21. Favorite thing to do on the weekend? _____

22. Where & when would you like to time-travel back to? _____

23. Where & when would you like to time-travel forward to? _____

24. What can you draw well? _____

25. ◯ Go with the flow   ◯ Stick to a routine?

26. Best type of cake? _____

27. ◯ Polka dots   ◯ Stripes   ◯ Plaid   ◯ Paisley?

28. What do you do after school? _____

29. ◯ Hang with friends   ◯ Go to a party?

30. How many times have you moved in your life? _____

What do I like to shop for?
super fun earrings!

1. Name? _____

2. How tall are you? _____

3. Camping in a ◯ cabin ◯ tent?

4. Kind of toothpaste you use? _____

5. What color is your bedroom? _____

6. Something that makes you nervous? _____

7. Make your bed every a.m.? ◯ Yes ◯ No

8. What did you do last night? _____

9. Biscuits with ◯ honey ◯ jam?

10. Awesome color combo? _____

11. Worse shopping for ◯ jeans ◯ bikini?

12. Number of children you would like someday? _____

13. ◯ Sunrise ◯ Sunset?

14. Coolest last name? _____

15. As a little kid, ◯ stuffed animal ◯ blankie?

16. ◯ Shower ◯ Bath?

17. Ever owned a goldfish? ◯ No ◯ Yes, _____
name

18. Cutest thing your pet does? _____

19. Something you refuse to eat? _____

20. Kind of bubblegum bubble blower are you? ◯ OK ◯ Highly skilled ◯ Awful

21. Fave pizza place? _____

22. What would be hard to give up? _____

23. Last thing you ate? _____

24. Push elevator buttons more than once? ◯ Never ◯ Always

25. Newest friend? _____

26. Love to see a ◯ volcano eruption ◯ solar eclipse?

27. Something you like to shop for? _____

28. What would you ask your future self? _____

29. ◯ Rollerblade ◯ Ice skate ◯ Skateboard ◯ None?

30. Afraid of spiders? ◯ YES! ◯ Nah

MY BIGGEST ? ABOUT LIFE?

WHAT ARE GNATS FOR?

1. Name? _____

2. Ever a teacher's pet? ◯ Yep ◯ No way!

3. Favorite candy? _____

4. ◯ Text ◯ IM ◯ Video-chat?

5. What makes you crazy? _____

6. Broken a body part? ◯ Nope ◯ Yep, broke my _____

7. Your biggest question about life? _____

8. Is your glass ½ ◯ full ◯ empty?

9. Most beautiful person (inside) you know? _____

10. How do you chill? _____

11. ◯ Social butterfly ◯ Wallflower?

12. Last accident/mess you caused? _____

13. Favorite relative? _____

14. Make your bed every a.m.? ◯ Yes ◯ No

15. Names of future children? _____

MY FAVE COLOR OF EYES R RAINBOW

16. ◯ Secret keeper ◯ Blabbermouth?

17. Favorite color of eyes? _____

18. ◯ Klutzy ◯ Sure-footed?

19. Latest wish? _____

20. Been sent to the principal's office? ◯ Yep ◯ Nope

21. ◯ Morning glory ◯ Night owl?

22. Favorite forest animal? _____

23. Birthmark? ◯ Yes ◯ No

24. Dream job? _____

25. ◯ Store-bought ◯ Homemade?

26. Something you don't understand? _____

27. Who would you be? ◯ Director ◯ Actor ◯ Makeup artist ◯ Set designer

28. What do u nosh on & drink at the movies? _____

29. What makes you cry? _____

30. Coolest color for a car? _____

coke or pepsi?

{ What is your full name? }

Nickname?

coke **OR** pepsi?

Favorite song?

Earliest memory?

Who do you call when you're upset?

○ TV ○ Book?	Last book you read?	○ **Milk** ○ **Dark** chocolate?
● Clean freak ● Total slob?	What kind of shoes are you wearing? Fave store?	○ **Beach** ○ **Mountains?** / Do you recycle? ○ yes ○ no
Do you wish on	● **Big Mac** ● **Whopper?** ● yes ● no	**Shirt** ● tucked ● out? Best gift you've ever received?
	Coolest car?	Best gift you've ever given?

Ever been stung by a jellyfish? ○ yes ○ no

Stupidest thing you've ever done ?

Best sitcom ever?

○ Dreamer
○ Doer?

Favorite doughnut?

_ _ _ _

1 word 2 describe U? 👉

Best cartoon ever? _

Last person you spoke to? _

Least favorite vegetable? _

Name of your very first friend? _ _ _ _ _ _ _ _ _ _ _ _ _ _ _ _ _ _ _

If u could, what would you change your name to? _ _ _ _ _ _ _ _ _ _ _ _ _

Favorite place you've visited? _

Ever pull an all-nighter?
○ yes ○ no

Believe in love at first sight?
○ yes ○ no

Been to NYC?
○ yes
○ no

Best pizza toppings? _ _ _ _ _ _ _ _
_ _ _ _ _ _ _ _ _ _

○ Night light
○ Completely dark?

scares you?

_ _ _ _ _ _

_ _ _ _

Been to **L.A.?**
○ yes ○ no

What

hamburger?
Gotta have double cheese

1. What are your initials? _____

2. ◯ Ice cubes ◯ Crushed ice?

3. What do you like on your burger? _____

4. Who do you admire the most? _____

5. How do your parents dance? ◯ Awesomely ◯ Terribly

6. Favorite food court place? _____

7. Worst appointment ever? ◯ Doctor ◯ Dentist

8. How old were you when you learned to swim? _____

9. ◯ Bagel ◯ Doughnut ◯ Croissant ◯ Cinnamon roll?

10. Favorite department store? _____

11. Know sign language? ◯ Yes ◯ No

12. Who taught you to ride a bike? _____

13. Been to the emergency room? ◯ Yes ◯ No

14. Last dream you remember? _____

15. Word or phrase you say a lot? _____

16. Worry ○ wart ○ free?

17. Worst movie ever? _____

18. ○ Reality show ○ Sitcom?

19. Best commercial? _____

20. Yummiest smoothie? _____

21. Fave brand of jeans? _____

22. Who would u be in the castle? ○ Queen ○ Princess ○ Knight ○ Jester

23. Game you liked as a kid? _____

24. Like to eat ○ a lot of different things ○ mainly fruits & veggies?

25. Advice for a 5-year-old? _____

26. Best type of movie? ○ Romance ○ Comedy ○ Scary ○ Action ○ Sci-Fi

27. Favorite author? _____

28. Most awesome cookie? _____

29. Tastiest fast food? _____

30. Time ○ drags ○ goes by too fast?

UF♡s? starg

1. First, middle, and last name? _____

2. Believe in UFOs? ◯ Yes! ◯ No!

3. What can't you live without? _____

4. Can you identify constellations? ◯ Yes ◯ No

5. Meanest thing you've done to a sibling?_____

6. ◯ Creamy   ◯ Crunchy peanut butter?

7. Take vitamins? ◯ Yeah ◯ Nah

8. Awesome little kid movie?_____

9. Someone or something you miss? _____

10. Floss? ◯ Yeah ◯ Nah

11. Believe in the Loch Ness monster? ◯ Yeah ◯ Nah

12. ◯ Apple ◯ Orange ◯ Pear ◯ Other _____?

13. WWYRH?* ◯ $50/week ◯ 3-day weekend

14. Any pets? ◯ No ◯ Yes, _____
                                          kinds

15. If yes to #14, names? _____

*Slang key WWYRH = What would you rather have

16. Best amusement park ride? _____

17. ◯ Train ◯ Plane ◯ Automobile?

18. How would you change your hair? _____

19. Museum of ◯ art ◯ natural history?

20. Believe in Bigfoot? ◯ Of course ◯ No way

21. Up to date on current news? ◯ Yes ◯ No

22. What's not fair? _____

23. ◯ Waffle cone ◯ Sugar cone ◯ Cup?

24. Favorite costume you've ever worn? _____

25. Which is worse? No ◯ TV ◯ Music

26. Best fairy tale? _____

27. ◯ Small purse ◯ Giant bag?

28. Ever have an imaginary friend? ◯ No ◯ Yes, _____

29. Can different foods touch on your plate? ◯ Yes ◯ No

30. Favorite pair of shoes? _____

coke or pepsi?

{ Name given at birth?

○ **Coffee**
○ **Tea?**

What do your friends call you?

Favorite holiday and why? ✔

What do you do when you're mad?

Favorite actor?

○ Radio ○ iPod
○ Other?

Favorite actress?

Ever won anything?
○ yes ○ no
↓ What?

Flower u love?

Oldest living relative?

Most annoying bug?

Best kind of music?

○   ○
person?

Ever been in love?
○ yes ○ no

What do you do on rainy days?

Nails:
○ Painted
○ Chipped
○ Fake
○ Bitten?

Wear painful shoes just because they're cute?
○ yes
○ no

○ **Tanning oil**
○ **Sunscreen?**

Have a secret you've never told?
○ yes ○ no

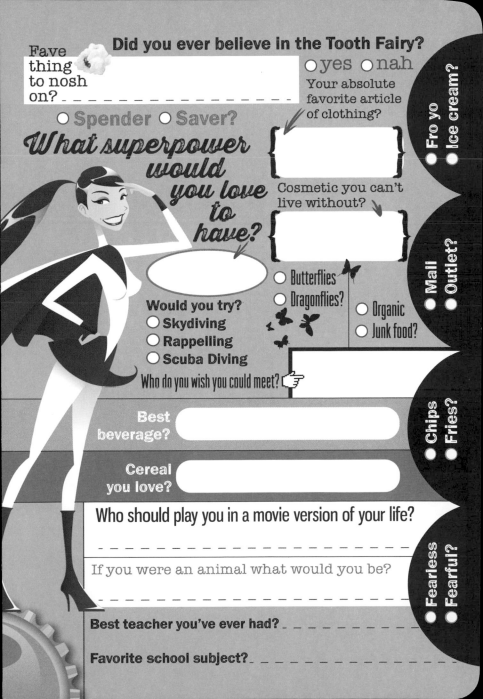

Fave thing to nosh on? _ _ _ _ _ _ _ _ _ _ _ _

Did you ever believe in the Tooth Fairy?

○ yes ○ nah

Your absolute favorite article of clothing?

○ Spender ○ Saver?

What superpower would you love to have?

Cosmetic you can't live without?

Would you try?
○ Skydiving
○ Rappelling
○ Scuba Diving

○ Butterflies
○ Dragonflies?

○ Organic
○ Junk food?

Who do you wish you could meet? ☞

Best beverage?

Cereal you love?

Who should play you in a movie version of your life?

_ _ _ _ _ _ _ _ _ _ _ _ _ _ _ _ _ _ _

If you were an animal what would you be?

_ _ _ _ _ _ _ _ _ _ _ _ _ _ _ _ _ _ _

Best teacher you've ever had? _ _ _ _ _ _ _ _ _ _ _

Favorite school subject? _ _ _ _ _ _ _ _ _ _

○ Fro yo ○ Ice cream?

○ Mall ○ Outlet?

○ Chips ○ Fries?

○ Fearless ○ Fearful?

BEST FRIEND
SINCE KINDERGARTEN

1. Name? _____

2. Where were you born? _____

3. Favorite picture book? _____

4. ◯ Hot dog ◯ Hamburger?

5. Invention you would love? _____

6. Friend you've had the longest? _____

7. ◯ White ◯ Wheat?

8. Best fashion era? ◯ 60s ◯ 70s ◯ 80s ◯ 90s ◯ Now

9. How many hours per day online? _____

10. How many hours per day texting? _____

11. What's scarier? ◯ Snake ◯ Shark

12. What do you always say "no" to? _____

13. Favorite food comes from which country? _____

14. Try to run away from home when you were little? ◯ Yes ◯ No

15. What are you not good at? _____

16. Something you would like to try? _____

17. ◯ Chocolate   ◯ Soy   ◯ Almond milk?

18. Friend who lives the farthest from you? _____

19. Where does #18 friend live? _____

20. Which could you give up? ◯ Email   ◯ Cell phone

21. ◯ Flip-flops   ◯ Strappy sandals?

22. Favorite season? _____ Why? _____

23. Read the ending before finishing a book? ◯ Yes   ◯ No

24. Who would you switch places with for one day? _____

25. ◯ Island cabana   ◯ European castle   ◯ Safari tent   ◯ Ski lodge?

26. What scared you as a little kid? _____

27. Favorite number? _____ Why? _____

28. ◯ Right-handed   ◯ Left-handed   ◯ Ambidextrous?

29. Color your toes are painted? _____

30. Ever needed stitches? ◯ No   ◯ Yes, for _____

I always find animals in the clouds

1. Name? _____

2. Birthday? _____

3. Something you can't stand the smell of? _____

4. Look for shapes in the clouds? ○ Yes ○ No

5. Coolest thing you learned this week?_____

6. What are you good at? _____

7. ○ Great vision ○ Glasses ○ Contacts?

8. Favorite take-out food? _____

9. Something you can't wait to do?_____

10. ○ Salty ○ Sweet?

11. Swallow anything by accident as a kid? ○ No ○ Yes, _____

12. Favorite accessory? _____

13. ○ Lone Ranger ○ Team Player?

14. ○ Bikini ○ One-piece?

15. Ever been snowed in? ○ No ○Yes

I dream of flying to exotic lands

16. Take pictures with ○ camera ○ phone?

17. Something you like to listen to? _____

18. ○ Tap ○ Bottled ○ Sparkling water?

19. What was your fave thing on the playground? _____

20. What would you love to see? _____

21. Favorite hot beverage? _____

22. Habit you wish you could change? _____

23. Are you a sore loser? ○ Yes ○ No

24. Yummiest ice cream flavor? _____

25. ○ Pilot ○ Navigator?

26. Who influences you the most? _____

27. Have you ever re-gifted? ○ No ○ Yes, _____

28. ○ Toilet-papered ○ Toilet-paperer?

29. What do you daydream about? _____

30. ○ Small talk ○ Deep conversation?

Travel back to the building of the pyramids

1. Nickname? _____

2. Shop ◯ alone ◯ with mom ◯ with friends?

3. ◯ Kill bugs ◯ Try to save them?

4. Favorite scent? _____

5. ◯ Manicure ◯ DIY nails?

6. Been in a talent show? ◯ No ◯ Yes, I _____

7. What's your current fave song about? _____

8. How do you like your popcorn? _____

9. ◯ Mild ◯ Medium ◯ Spicy?

10. Magazine you love? _____

11. ◯ Details ◯ Big picture?

12. Favorite comfort food? _____

13. ◯ Super trendy ◯ Totally casual?

14. Best friend in kindergarten? _____

15. What can't you bear the sound of? _____

16. ◯ Gold ◯ Silver ◯ Costume jewelry?

17. Coolest first name? _____

18. Favorite hangout? _____

19. Ever think there was a monster under your bed? ◯ Yes ◯ No

20. ◯ Brownies ◯ Chocolate chip cookies?

21. Favorite thing to do on the weekend? _____

22. Where & when would you like to time-travel back to? _____

23. Where & when would you like to time-travel forward to? _____

24. What can you draw well? _____

25. ◯ Go with the flow ◯ Stick to a routine?

26. Best type of cake? _____

27. ◯ Polka dots ◯ Stripes ◯ Plaid ◯ Paisley?

28. What do you do after school? _____

29. ◯ Hang with friends ◯ Go to a party?

30. How many times have you moved in your life? _____

What do I like to shop for?

super fun earrings!

1. Name? _____

2. How tall are you? _____

3. Camping in a ◯ cabin ◯ tent?

4. Kind of toothpaste you use? _____

5. What color is your bedroom? _____

6. Something that makes you nervous? _____

7. Make your bed every a.m.? ◯ Yes ◯ No

8. What did you do last night? _____

9. Biscuits with ◯ honey ◯ jam?

10. Awesome color combo? _____

11. Worse shopping for ◯ jeans ◯ bikini?

12. Number of children you would like someday? _____

13. ◯ Sunrise ◯ Sunset?

14. Coolest last name? _____

15. As a little kid, ◯ stuffed animal ◯ blankie?

16. ⃝ Shower ⃝ Bath?

17. Ever owned a goldfish? ⃝ No ⃝ Yes, _____
name

18. Cutest thing your pet does? _____

19. Something you refuse to eat? _____

20. Kind of bubblegum bubble blower are you? ⃝ OK ⃝ Highly skilled ⃝ Awful

21. Fave pizza place? _____

22. What would be hard to give up? _____

23. Last thing you ate? _____

24. Push elevator buttons more than once? ⃝ Never ⃝ Always

25. Newest friend? _____

26. Love to see a ⃝ volcano eruption ⃝ solar eclipse?

27. Something you like to shop for? _____

28. What would you ask your future self? _____

29. ⃝ Rollerblade ⃝ Ice skate ⃝ Skateboard ⃝ None?

30. Afraid of spiders? ⃝ YES! ⃝ Nah

MY BIGGEST **?** ABOUT LIFE?

1. Name? _____

2. Ever a teacher's pet? ◯ Yep ◯ No way!

3. Favorite candy? _____

4. ◯ Text ◯ IM ◯ Video-chat?

5. What makes you crazy? _____

6. Broken a body part? ◯ Nope ◯ Yep, broke my _____

7. Your biggest question about life? _____

8. Is your glass ½ ◯ full ◯ empty?

9. Most beautiful person (inside) you know? _____

10. How do you chill? _____

11. ◯ Social butterfly ◯ Wallflower?

12. Last accident/mess you caused? _____

13. Favorite relative? _____

14. Make your bed every a.m.? ◯ Yes ◯ No

15. Names of future children? _____

16. ◯ Secret keeper ◯ Blabbermouth?

17. Favorite color of eyes? _____

18. ◯ Klutzy ◯ Sure-footed?

19. Latest wish? _____

20. Been sent to the principal's office? ◯ Yep ◯ Nope

21. ◯ Morning glory ◯ Night owl?

22. Favorite forest animal? _____

23. Birthmark? ◯ Yes ◯ No

24. Dream job? _____

25. ◯ Store-bought ◯ Homemade?

26. Something you don't understand? _____

27. Who would you be? ◯ Director ◯ Actor ◯ Makeup artist ◯ Set designer

28. What do u nosh on & drink at the movies? _____

29. What makes you cry? _____

30. Coolest color for a car? _____

coke or pepsi?

{ What is your full name? } _____ Nickname? 👆

coke OR **pepsi?**

Favorite song? _____

Earliest memory? _____

Who do you call when you're upset? ▷ _____

○ **TV** ○ **Book?**	Last book you read? _____	○ **Milk** ○ **Dark** chocolate?
● Clean freak ● Total slob?	What kind of shoes are you wearing? _____ Fave store?	○ **Beach** ○ **Mountains?**	Do you recycle? ○ yes ○ no

Do you wish on

● **Big Mac** ● **Whopper?**

● yes ● no

Coolest car? _____

Shirt ● tucked ● out?

Best gift you've ever received? _____

Best gift you've ever given? _____

Ever been stung by a jellyfish?
○ yes
○ no

Stupidest thing you've ever done ?

Best sitcom ever?

○ Dreamer
○ Doer?

Favorite doughnut?

1 word 2 describe U?

Best cartoon ever? _

Last person you spoke to? _ _ _ _ _ _ _ _ _ _ _ _ _ _ _ _ _ _ _

Least favorite vegetable? _ _ _ _ _ _ _ _ _ _ _ _ _ _ _ _ _ _ _

Name of your very first friend? _ _ _ _ _ _ _ _ _ _ _ _ _ _ _ _

If u could, what would you change your name to? _ _ _ _ _ _ _ _

Favorite place you've visited? _ _ _ _ _ _ _ _ _ _ _ _ _ _ _ _

Ever pull an all-nighter?
○ yes ○ no

Believe in love at first sight?
○ yes ○ no

Been to NYC?
○ yes
○ no

Best pizza toppings? _ _ _ _ _ _ _ _

_ _ _ _ _ _ _ _ _ _

○ Night light
○ Completely dark?

scares you?

Been to L.A.?
○ yes ○ no

What
_ _ _ _ _ _ _
_ _ _ _ _ _ _

Gotta have double cheese

hamburger?

1. What are your initials? _____

2. ◯ Ice cubes   ◯ Crushed ice?

3. What do you like on your burger? _____

4. Who do you admire the most? _____

5. How do your parents dance?   ◯ Awesomely   ◯ Terribly

6. Favorite food court place? _____

7. Worst appointment ever?   ◯ Doctor   ◯ Dentist

8. How old were you when you learned to swim? _____

9. ◯ Bagel   ◯ Doughnut   ◯ Croissant   ◯ Cinnamon roll?

10. Favorite department store? _____

11. Know sign language?   ◯ Yes   ◯ No

12. Who taught you to ride a bike? _____

13. Been to the emergency room?   ◯ Yes   ◯ No

14. Last dream you remember? _____

15. Word or phrase you say a lot? _____

chocolate chip
Fave cookie is

16. Worry ○ wart ○ free?

17. Worst movie ever? _____

18. ○ Reality show ○ Sitcom?

19. Best commercial? _____

20. Yummiest smoothie? _____

21. Fave brand of jeans? _____

22. Who would u be in the castle? ○ Queen ○ Princess ○ Knight ○ Jester

23. Game you liked as a kid? _____

24. Like to eat ○ a lot of different things ○ mainly fruits & veggies?

25. Advice for a 5-year-old? _____

26. Best type of movie? ○ Romance ○ Comedy ○ Scary ○ Action ○ Sci-Fi

27. Favorite author? _____

28. Most awesome cookie? _____

29. Tastiest fast food? _____

30. Time ○ drags ○ goes by too fast?

1. First, middle, and last name? _____

2. Believe in UFOs? ◯ Yes! ◯ No!

3. What can't you live without? _____

4. Can you identify constellations? ◯ Yes ◯ No

5. Meanest thing you've done to a sibling?_____

6. ◯ Creamy ◯ Crunchy peanut butter?

7. Take vitamins? ◯ Yeah ◯ Nah

8. Awesome little kid movie?_____

9. Someone or something you miss? _____

10. Floss? ◯ Yeah ◯ Nah

11. Believe in the Loch Ness monster? ◯ Yeah ◯ Nah

12. ◯ Apple ◯ Orange ◯ Pear ◯ Other _____?

13. WWYRH?* ◯ $50/week ◯ 3-day weekend

14. Any pets? ◯ No ◯ Yes, _____
kinds

15. If yes to #14, names? _____

* *Slang key* WWYRH = What would you rather have

Yes way!
oh, please

16. Best amusement park ride? _____

17. ◯ Train ◯ Plane ◯ Automobile?

18. How would you change your hair? _____

19. Museum of ◯ art ◯ natural history?

20. Believe in Bigfoot? ◯ Of course ◯ No way

21. Up to date on current news? ◯ Yes ◯ No

22. What's not fair? _____

23. ◯ Waffle cone ◯ Sugar cone ◯ Cup?

24. Favorite costume you've ever worn? _____

25. Which is worse? No ◯ TV ◯ Music

26. Best fairy tale? _____

27. ◯ Small purse ◯ Giant bag?

28. Ever have an imaginary friend? ◯ No ◯ Yes, _____

29. Can different foods touch on your plate? ◯ Yes ◯ No

30. Favorite pair of shoes? _____

coke or pepsi?

{ Name given at birth? }

○ **Coffee**
○ **Tea?**

What do your friends call you? ➤

Favorite holiday and why? ✔

What do you do when you're mad?

Favorite actor?

○ Radio ○ iPod ○ Other?

Favorite actress?

Ever won anything?
○ yes ○ no
↓ What?

Flower u love?

Oldest living relative?

Most annoying bug?

Best kind of music?

○ 🦖 ○ 🐆 **person?**

What do you do on rainy days?

Ever been in love?
○ yes ○ no

Nails:
○ Painted
○ Chipped
○ Fake
○ Bitten?

○ **Tanning oil**
○ **Sunscreen?**

Wear painful shoes just because they're cute?
○ yes
○ no

Have a secret you've never told?
○ yes ○ no

Fave thing to nosh on?

Did you ever believe in the Tooth Fairy? ○ yes ○ nah

Your absolute favorite article of clothing?

○ Spender ○ Saver?

What superpower would you love to have?

Cosmetic you can't live without?

Would you try?
○ Skydiving
○ Rappelling
○ Scuba Diving

○ Butterflies
○ Dragonflies?

○ Organic
○ Junk food?

Who do you wish you could meet?

Best beverage?

Cereal you love?

Who should play you in a movie version of your life?

If you were an animal what would you be?

Best teacher you've ever had?

Favorite school subject?

○ Fro yo
○ Ice cream?

○ Mall
○ Outlet?

○ Chips
○ Fries?

○ Fearless
○ Fearful?

BEST FRIEND
SINCE KINDERGARTEN

1. Name? _____

2. Where were you born? _____

3. Favorite picture book? _____

4. ◯ Hot dog   ◯ Hamburger?

5. Invention you would love? _____

6. Friend you've had the longest? _____

7. ◯ White   ◯ Wheat?

8. Best fashion era?   ◯ 60s ◯ 70s ◯ 80s ◯ 90s ◯ Now

9. How many hours per day online? _____

10. How many hours per day texting? _____

11. What's scarier? ◯ Snake   ◯ Shark

12. What do you always say "no" to? _____

13. Favorite food comes from which country? _____

14. Try to run away from home when you were little? ◯ Yes ◯ No

15. What are you not good at? _____

FARAWAY
FRIEND

SO MANY MILES ...

16. Something you would like to try? _____

17. ⚪ Chocolate ⚪ Soy ⚪ Almond milk?

18. Friend who lives the farthest from you? _____

19. Where does #18 friend live? _____

20. Which could you give up? ⚪ Email ⚪ Cell phone

21. ⚪ Flip-flops ⚪ Strappy sandals?

22. Favorite season? _____ Why? _____

23. Read the ending before finishing a book? ⚪ Yes ⚪ No

24. Who would you switch places with for one day? _____

25. ⚪ Island cabana ⚪ European castle ⚪ Safari tent ⚪ Ski lodge?

26. What scared you as a little kid? _____

27. Favorite number? _____ Why? _____

28. ⚪ Right-handed ⚪ Left-handed ⚪ Ambidextrous?

29. Color your toes are painted? _____

30. Ever needed stitches? ⚪ No ⚪ Yes, for _____

I always find animals in the clouds

1. Name? _____

2. Birthday? _____

3. Something you can't stand the smell of? _____

4. Look for shapes in the clouds? ○ Yes ○ No

5. Coolest thing you learned this week? _____

6. What are you good at? _____

7. ○ Great vision ○ Glasses ○ Contacts?

8. Favorite take-out food? _____

9. Something you can't wait to do? _____

10. ○ Salty ○ Sweet?

11. Swallow anything by accident as a kid? ○ No ○ Yes, _____

12. Favorite accessory? _____

13. ○ Lone Ranger ○ Team Player?

14. ○ Bikini ○ One-piece?

15. Ever been snowed in? ○ No ○ Yes

16. Take pictures with ◯ camera ◯ phone?

17. Something you like to listen to? _____

18. ◯ Tap ◯ Bottled ◯ Sparkling water?

19. What was your fave thing on the playground? _____

20. What would you love to see? _____

21. Favorite hot beverage? _____

22. Habit you wish you could change?_____

23. Are you a sore loser? ◯ Yes ◯ No

24. Yummiest ice cream flavor? _____

25. ◯ Pilot ◯ Navigator?

26. Who influences you the most? _____

27. Have you ever re-gifted? ◯ No ◯ Yes, _____

28. ◯ Toilet-papered ◯ Toilet-paperer?

29. What do you daydream about? _____

30. ◯ Small talk ◯ Deep conversation?

Travel back to the building of the pyramids

1. Nickname? _____

2. Shop ○ alone ○ with mom ○ with friends?

3. ○ Kill bugs ○ Try to save them?

4. Favorite scent? _____

5. ○ Manicure ○ DIY nails?

6. Been in a talent show? ○ No ○ Yes, I _____

7. What's your current fave song about? _____

8. How do you like your popcorn? _____

9. ○ Mild ○ Medium ○ Spicy?

10. Magazine you love? _____

11. ○ Details ○ Big picture?

12. Favorite comfort food? _____

13. ○ Super trendy ○ Totally casual?

14. Best friend in kindergarten? _____

15. What can't you bear the sound of? _____

16. ◯ Gold   ◯ Silver   ◯ Costume jewelry?

17. Coolest first name? _____

18. Favorite hangout? _____

19. Ever think there was a monster under your bed? ◯ Yes ◯ No

20. ◯ Brownies   ◯ Chocolate chip cookies?

21. Favorite thing to do on the weekend? _____

22. Where & when would you like to time-travel back to? _____

23. Where & when would you like to time-travel forward to? _____

24. What can you draw well? _____

25. ◯ Go with the flow   ◯ Stick to a routine?

26. Best type of cake? _____

27. ◯ Polka dots   ◯ Stripes   ◯ Plaid   ◯ Paisley?

28. What do you do after school? _____

29. ◯ Hang with friends   ◯ Go to a party?

30. How many times have you moved in your life? _____

What do I like to shop for?

super fun earrings!

1. Name? _____

2. How tall are you? _____

3. Camping in a ◯ cabin ◯ tent?

4. Kind of toothpaste you use? _____

5. What color is your bedroom? _____

6. Something that makes you nervous? _____

7. Make your bed every a.m.? ◯ Yes ◯ No

8. What did you do last night? _____

9. Biscuits with ◯ honey ◯ jam?

10. Awesome color combo? _____

11. Worse shopping for ◯ jeans ◯ bikini?

12. Number of children you would like someday? _____

13. ◯ Sunrise ◯ Sunset?

14. Coolest last name? _____

15. As a little kid, ◯ stuffed animal ◯ blankie?

16. ◯ Shower ◯ Bath?

17. Ever owned a goldfish? ◯ No ◯ Yes, _____
name

18. Cutest thing your pet does? _____

19. Something you refuse to eat? _____

20. Kind of bubblegum bubble blower are you? ◯ OK ◯ Highly skilled ◯ Awful

21. Fave pizza place? _____

22. What would be hard to give up? _____

23. Last thing you ate? _____

24. Push elevator buttons more than once? ◯ Never ◯ Always

25. Newest friend? _____

26. Love to see a ◯ volcano eruption ◯ solar eclipse?

27. Something you like to shop for? _____

28. What would you ask your future self? _____

29. ◯ Rollerblade ◯ Ice skate ◯ Skateboard ◯ None?

30. Afraid of spiders? ◯ YES! ◯ Nah

MY BIGGEST ? ABOUT LIFE?

WHAT ARE GNATS FOR?

1. Name? _____

2. Ever a teacher's pet? ◯ Yep ◯ No way!

3. Favorite candy? _____

4. ◯ Text ◯ IM ◯ Video-chat?

5. What makes you crazy? _____

6. Broken a body part? ◯ Nope ◯ Yep, broke my _____

7. Your biggest question about life? _____

8. Is your glass ½ ◯ full ◯ empty?

9. Most beautiful person (inside) you know? _____

10. How do you chill? _____

11. ◯ Social butterfly ◯ Wallflower?

12. Last accident/mess you caused? _____

13. Favorite relative? _____

14. Make your bed every a.m.? ◯ Yes ◯ No

15. Names of future children? _____

MY FAVE COLOR OF EYES R RAINBOW

16. ○ Secret keeper   ○ Blabbermouth?

17. Favorite color of eyes? _____

18. ○ Klutzy   ○ Sure-footed?

19. Latest wish? _____

20. Been sent to the principal's office? ○ Yep   ○ Nope

21. ○ Morning glory   ○ Night owl?

22. Favorite forest animal? _____

23. Birthmark?   ○ Yes   ○ No

24. Dream job? _____

25. ○ Store-bought   ○ Homemade?

26. Something you don't understand? _____

27. Who would you be? ○ Director ○ Actor ○ Makeup artist ○ Set designer

28. What do u nosh on & drink at the movies? _____

29. What makes you cry? _____

30. Coolest color for a car? _____

coke or pepsi?

{ What is your full name? _____ }

coke OR **pepsi?**

Favorite song?

_____

🧠 **Earliest memory?** _____

Who do you call when you're upset? ▷ _____

○ **TV** ○ **Bo ok?**	Last book you read? _____	○ **Milk** ○ **Dark** chocolate?
● Clean freak ● Total slob?	What kind of shoes are you wearing? _____ Fave store?	○ **Beach** ○ **Moun tains?** / Do you recycle? ○ yes ○ no

Do you wish on

○ **Big Mac** ○ **Whopper?**

○ yes ○ no

Coolest car? _____

Shirt ● tucked ● out?

Best gift you've ever received? _____

Best gift you've ever given? _____

Ever been stung by a jellyfish?
○ yes
○ no

Stupidest thing you've ever done ?

Best sitcom ever?

○ Dreamer
○ Doer?

Favorite doughnut?
_ _ _ _ _

1 word 2 describe U?

Best cartoon ever? _ _ _ _ _ _ _ _ _ _ _ _ _ _

Last person you spoke to? _ _ _ _ _ _ _ _ _ _ _ _ _ _

Least favorite vegetable? _ _ _ _ _ _ _ _ _ _ _ _ _ _

Name of your very first friend? _ _ _ _ _ _ _ _ _ _ _ _ _ _

If u could, what would you change your name to? _ _ _ _ _ _ _ _ _ _ _ _ _ _

Favorite place you've visited? _ _ _ _ _ _ _ _ _ _ _ _ _ _

Ever pull an all-nighter?
○ yes ○ no

Believe in love at first sight?
○ yes ○ no

Been to NYC?
○ yes
○ no

Best pizza toppings? _ _ _ _ _ _ _
_ _ _ _ _ _ _

● Night light
● Completely dark?

Been to L.A.?
○ yes ○ no

What scares you?
_ _ _ _
_ _ _ _

hamburger? ←
Gotta have double cheese

1. What are your initials? _____

2. ○ Ice cubes ○ Crushed ice?

3. What do you like on your burger? _____

4. Who do you admire the most? _____

5. How do your parents dance? ○ Awesomely ○ Terribly

6. Favorite food court place? _____

7. Worst appointment ever? ○ Doctor ○ Dentist

8. How old were you when you learned to swim? _____

9. ○ Bagel ○ Doughnut ○ Croissant ○ Cinnamon roll?

10. Favorite department store? _____

11. Know sign language? ○ Yes ○ No

12. Who taught you to ride a bike? _____

13. Been to the emergency room? ○ Yes ○ No

14. Last dream you remember? _____

15. Word or phrase you say a lot? _____

→ chocolate chip
Fave cookie is

16. Worry ◯ wart ◯ free?

17. Worst movie ever? _____

18. ◯ Reality show ◯ Sitcom?

19. Best commercial? _____

20. Yummiest smoothie? _____

21. Fave brand of jeans? _____

22. Who would u be in the castle? ◯ Queen ◯ Princess ◯ Knight ◯ Jester

23. Game you liked as a kid? _____

24. Like to eat ◯ a lot of different things ◯ mainly fruits & veggies?

25. Advice for a 5-year-old? _____

26. Best type of movie? ◯ Romance ◯ Comedy ◯ Scary ◯ Action ◯ Sci-Fi

27. Favorite author? _____

28. Most awesome cookie? _____

29. Tastiest fast food? _____

30. Time ◯ drags ◯ goes by too fast?

1. First, middle, and last name? _____

2. Believe in UFOs? ◯ Yes! ◯ No!

3. What can't you live without? _____

4. Can you identify constellations? ◯ Yes ◯ No

5. Meanest thing you've done to a sibling?_____

6. ◯ Creamy ◯ Crunchy peanut butter?

7. Take vitamins? ◯ Yeah ◯ Nah

8. Awesome little kid movie?_____

9. Someone or something you miss?_____

10. Floss? ◯ Yeah ◯ Nah

11. Believe in the Loch Ness monster? ◯ Yeah ◯ Nah

12. ◯ Apple ◯ Orange ◯ Pear ◯ Other _____?

13. WWYRH?* ◯ $50/week ◯ 3-day weekend

14. Any pets? ◯ No ◯ Yes, _____
kinds

15. If yes to #14, names? _____

* *Slang key* WWYRH = What would you rather have

16. Best amusement park ride? _____

17. ○ Train ○ Plane ○ Automobile?

18. How would you change your hair? _____

19. Museum of ○ art ○ natural history?

20. Believe in Bigfoot? ○ Of course ○ No way

21. Up to date on current news? ○ Yes ○ No

22. What's not fair? _____

23. ○ Waffle cone ○ Sugar cone ○ Cup?

24. Favorite costume you've ever worn? _____

25. Which is worse? No ○ TV ○ Music

26. Best fairy tale? _____

27. ○ Small purse ○ Giant bag?

28. Ever have an imaginary friend? ○ No ○ Yes, _____

29. Can different foods touch on your plate? ○ Yes ○ No

30. Favorite pair of shoes? _____

coke or pepsi?

Name given at birth?

○ **Coffee**
○ **Tea?**

What do your friends call you?

Favorite holiday and why? ✔

What do you do when you're mad?

Favorite actor?

○ Radio ○ iPod
○ Other?

Favorite actress?

Ever won anything?
○ yes ○ no
↓ What?

Flower u love? _ _ _ _ _ _ _ _ _

Oldest living relative? _ _ _ _ _ _ _

Most annoying bug? _ _ _ _ _ _ _ _

Best kind of music? _ _ _ _ _ _ _ _

○ 🐕 ○ 🐈
person?

What do you do on rainy days?

Ever been in love?
○ yes ○ no

Nails:
○ Painted
○ Chipped
○ Fake
○ Bitten?

Wear painful shoes just because they're cute?
○ yes
○ no

○ **Tanning oil**
○ **Sunscreen?**

Have a secret you've never told?
○ yes ○ no

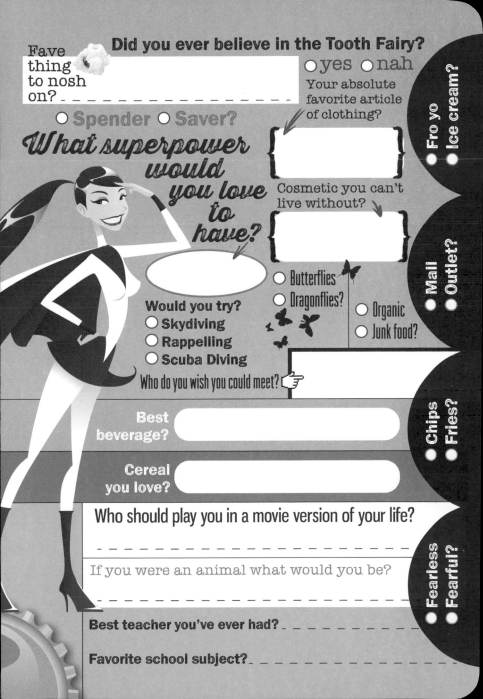

Fave thing to nosh on? _

Did you ever believe in the Tooth Fairy?
○ yes ○ nah

Your absolute favorite article of clothing?

Fro yo ○ Ice cream? ○

○ Spender ○ Saver?

What superpower would you love to have?

Cosmetic you can't live without?

Mall ○ Outlet? ○

Would you try?
○ Skydiving
○ Rappelling
○ Scuba Diving

○ Butterflies
○ Dragonflies?

○ Organic
○ Junk food?

Who do you wish you could meet? ☞

Best beverage?

Chips ○ Fries? ○

Cereal you love?

Who should play you in a movie version of your life?
_ _

If you were an animal what would you be?
_ _

Fearless ○ Fearful? ○

Best teacher you've ever had? _ _ _ _ _ _ _ _ _ _

Favorite school subject? _ _ _ _ _ _ _ _ _ _ _ _ _

BEST FRIEND
SINCE KINDERGARTEN

1. Name? _____

2. Where were you born? _____

3. Favorite picture book? _____

4. ◯ Hot dog ◯ Hamburger?

5. Invention you would love? _____

6. Friend you've had the longest? _____

7. ◯ White ◯ Wheat?

8. Best fashion era? ◯ 60s ◯ 70s ◯ 80s ◯ 90s ◯ Now

9. How many hours per day online? _____

10. How many hours per day texting? _____

11. What's scarier? ◯ Snake ◯ Shark

12. What do you always say "no" to? _____

13. Favorite food comes from which country? _____

14. Try to run away from home when you were little? ◯ Yes ◯ No

15. What are you not good at? _____

16. Something you would like to try? _____

17. ◯ Chocolate ◯ Soy ◯ Almond milk?

18. Friend who lives the farthest from you? _____

19. Where does #18 friend live? _____

20. Which could you give up? ◯ Email ◯ Cell phone

21. ◯ Flip-flops ◯ Strappy sandals?

22. Favorite season? _____ Why? _____

23. Read the ending before finishing a book? ◯ Yes ◯ No

24. Who would you switch places with for one day? _____

25. ◯ Island cabana ◯ European castle ◯ Safari tent ◯ Ski lodge?

26. What scared you as a little kid? _____

27. Favorite number? _____ Why? _____

28. ◯ Right-handed ◯ Left-handed ◯ Ambidextrous?

29. Color your toes are painted? _____

30. Ever needed stitches? ◯ No ◯ Yes, for _____

I always find animals in the clouds

1. Name? _____

2. Birthday? _____

3. Something you can't stand the smell of? _____

4. Look for shapes in the clouds? ◯ Yes ◯ No

5. Coolest thing you learned this week? _____

6. What are you good at? _____

7. ◯ Great vision ◯ Glasses ◯ Contacts?

8. Favorite take-out food? _____

9. Something you can't wait to do? _____

10. ◯ Salty ◯ Sweet?

11. Swallow anything by accident as a kid? ◯ No ◯ Yes, _____

12. Favorite accessory? _____

13. ◯ Lone Ranger ◯ Team Player?

14. ◯ Bikini ◯ One-piece?

15. Ever been snowed in? ◯ No ◯ Yes

16. Take pictures with ◯ camera ◯ phone?

17. Something you like to listen to? _____

18. ◯ Tap ◯ Bottled ◯ Sparkling water?

19. What was your fave thing on the playground? _____

20. What would you love to see? _____

21. Favorite hot beverage? _____

22. Habit you wish you could change? _____

23. Are you a sore loser? ◯ Yes ◯ No

24. Yummiest ice cream flavor? _____

25. ◯ Pilot ◯ Navigator?

26. Who influences you the most? _____

27. Have you ever re-gifted? ◯ No ◯ Yes, _____

28. ◯ Toilet-papered ◯ Toilet-paperer?

29. What do you daydream about? _____

30. ◯ Small talk ◯ Deep conversation?

Travel back to the building of the pyramids

1. Nickname? _____

2. Shop ◯ alone ◯ with mom ◯ with friends?

3. ◯ Kill bugs ◯ Try to save them?

4. Favorite scent? _____

5. ◯ Manicure ◯ DIY nails?

6. Been in a talent show? ◯ No ◯ Yes, I _____

7. What's your current fave song about? _____

8. How do you like your popcorn? _____

9. ◯ Mild ◯ Medium ◯ Spicy?

10. Magazine you love? _____

11. ◯ Details ◯ Big picture?

12. Favorite comfort food? _____

13. ◯ Super trendy ◯ Totally casual?

14. Best friend in kindergarten? _____

15. What can't you bear the sound of? _____

16. ◯ Gold   ◯ Silver   ◯ Costume jewelry?

17. Coolest first name? _____

18. Favorite hangout? _____

19. Ever think there was a monster under your bed? ◯ Yes ◯ No

20. ◯ Brownies   ◯ Chocolate chip cookies?

21. Favorite thing to do on the weekend? _____

22. Where & when would you like to time-travel back to? _____

23. Where & when would you like to time-travel forward to? _____

24. What can you draw well? _____

25. ◯ Go with the flow   ◯ Stick to a routine?

26. Best type of cake? _____

27. ◯ Polka dots   ◯ Stripes   ◯ Plaid   ◯ Paisley?

28. What do you do after school? _____

29. ◯ Hang with friends   ◯ Go to a party?

30. How many times have you moved in your life? _____

What do I like to shop for?

super fun earrings!

1. Name? _____

2. How tall are you? _____

3. Camping in a ◯ cabin ◯ tent?

4. Kind of toothpaste you use? _____

5. What color is your bedroom? _____

6. Something that makes you nervous? _____

7. Make your bed every a.m.? ◯ Yes ◯ No

8. What did you do last night? _____

9. Biscuits with ◯ honey ◯ jam?

10. Awesome color combo? _____

11. Worse shopping for ◯ jeans ◯ bikini?

12. Number of children you would like someday? _____

13. ◯ Sunrise ◯ Sunset?

14. Coolest last name? _____

15. As a little kid, ◯ stuffed animal ◯ blankie?

16. ○ Shower ○ Bath?

17. Ever owned a goldfish? ○ No ○ Yes, _____
name

18. Cutest thing your pet does? _____

19. Something you refuse to eat? _____

20. Kind of bubblegum bubble blower are you? ○ OK ○ Highly skilled ○ Awful

21. Fave pizza place? _____

22. What would be hard to give up? _____

23. Last thing you ate? _____

24. Push elevator buttons more than once? ○ Never ○ Always

25. Newest friend? _____

26. Love to see a ○ volcano eruption ○ solar eclipse?

27. Something you like to shop for? _____

28. What would you ask your future self? _____

29. ○ Rollerblade ○ Ice skate ○ Skateboard ○ None?

30. Afraid of spiders? ○ YES! ○ Nah

MY BIGGEST ? ABOUT LIFE?

WHAT ARE GNATS FOR?

1. Name? _____

2. Ever a teacher's pet? ◯ Yep ◯ No way!

3. Favorite candy? _____

4. ◯ Text ◯ IM ◯ Video-chat?

5. What makes you crazy? _____

6. Broken a body part? ◯ Nope ◯ Yep, broke my _____

7. Your biggest question about life? _____

8. Is your glass ½ ◯ full ◯ empty?

9. Most beautiful person (inside) you know? _____

10. How do you chill? _____

11. ◯ Social butterfly ◯ Wallflower?

12. Last accident/mess you caused? _____

13. Favorite relative? _____

14. Make your bed every a.m.? ◯ Yes ◯ No

15. Names of future children? _____

16. ◯ Secret keeper ◯ Blabbermouth?

17. Favorite color of eyes? _____

18. ◯ Klutzy ◯ Sure-footed?

19. Latest wish? _____

20. Been sent to the principal's office? ◯ Yep ◯ Nope

21. ◯ Morning glory ◯ Night owl?

22. Favorite forest animal? _____

23. Birthmark? ◯ Yes ◯ No

24. Dream job? _____

25. ◯ Store-bought ◯ Homemade?

26. Something you don't understand? _____

27. Who would you be? ◯ Director ◯ Actor ◯ Makeup artist ◯ Set designer

28. What do u nosh on & drink at the movies? _____

29. What makes you cry? _____

30. Coolest color for a car? _____

coke or pepsi?

{ What is your full name? } Nickname?

coke OR **pepsi?**

Favorite song?

🧠 Earliest memory?

Who do you call when you're upset?

○ **TV**
○ **Book?**

Last book you read?

○ **Milk** ○ **Dark** chocolate?

● Clean freak
● Total slob?

What kind of shoes are you wearing?

Fave store?

○ **Beach**
○ **Mountains?**

Do you recycle?
○ yes
○ no

Do you wish on

○ **Big Mac**
○ **Whopper?**

○ yes
○ no

Shirt
● tucked ● out?

Best gift you've ever received?

Best gift you've ever given?

Coolest car?

Ever been stung by a jellyfish? ○ yes ○ no

Stupidest thing you've ever done❓

Best sitcom ever?

○ Dreamer
○ Doer?

Favorite doughnut?
_ _ _ _ _

1 word 2 describe U? 👉

Best cartoon ever? _

Last person you spoke to? _

Least favorite vegetable? _

Name of your very first friend? _ _ _ _ _ _ _ _ _ _ _ _ _ _ _ _ _ _ _

If u could, what would you change your name to? _ _ _ _ _ _ _ _ _ _ _

Favorite place you've visited? _ _ _ _ _ _ _ _ _ _ _ _ _ _ _ _ _ _

Ever pull an all-nighter?
○ yes ○ no

Believe in love at first sight?
○ yes ○ no

Been to **NYC?**
○ yes
○ no

Best pizza toppings? _

○ Night light
○ Completely dark?

scares you?

Been to **L.A.?**
○ yes ○ no

What
_ _ _ _ _
_ _ _ _ _

hamburger? ←

Gotta have double cheese

1. What are your initials? _____

2. ○ Ice cubes ○ Crushed ice?

3. What do you like on your burger? _____

4. Who do you admire the most? _____

5. How do your parents dance? ○ Awesomely ○ Terribly

6. Favorite food court place? _____

7. Worst appointment ever? ○ Doctor ○ Dentist

8. How old were you when you learned to swim? _____

9. ○ Bagel ○ Doughnut ○ Croissant ○ Cinnamon roll?

10. Favorite department store? _____

11. Know sign language? ○ Yes ○ No

12. Who taught you to ride a bike? _____

13. Been to the emergency room? ○ Yes ○ No

14. Last dream you remember? _____

15. Word or phrase you say a lot? _____

16. Worry ○ wart ○ free?

17. Worst movie ever? _____

18. ○ Reality show ○ Sitcom?

19. Best commercial? _____

20. Yummiest smoothie? _____

21. Fave brand of jeans? _____

22. Who would u be in the castle? ○ Queen ○ Princess ○ Knight ○ Jester

23. Game you liked as a kid? _____

24. Like to eat ○ a lot of different things ○ mainly fruits & veggies?

25. Advice for a 5-year-old? _____

26. Best type of movie? ○ Romance ○ Comedy ○ Scary ○ Action ○ Sci-Fi

27. Favorite author? _____

28. Most awesome cookie? _____

29. Tastiest fast food? _____

30. Time ○ drags ○ goes by too fast?

UF♡s? stars

1. First, middle, and last name? _____

2. Believe in UFOs? ◯ Yes! ◯ No!

3. What can't you live without? _____

4. Can you identify constellations? ◯ Yes ◯ No

5. Meanest thing you've done to a sibling?_____

6. ◯ Creamy ◯ Crunchy peanut butter?

7. Take vitamins? ◯ Yeah ◯ Nah

8. Awesome little kid movie?_____

9. Someone or something you miss? _____

10. Floss? ◯ Yeah ◯ Nah

11. Believe in the Loch Ness monster? ◯ Yeah ◯ Nah

12. ◯ Apple ◯ Orange ◯ Pear ◯ Other _____ ?

13. WWYRH?* ◯ $50/week ◯ 3-day weekend

14. Any pets? ◯ No ◯ Yes, _____
kinds

15. If yes to #14, names? _____

* *Slang key* WWYRH = What would you rather have

azing *Yes way!*

oh, please

16. Best amusement park ride? _____

17. ◯ Train ◯ Plane ◯ Automobile?

18. How would you change your hair? _____

19. Museum of ◯ art ◯ natural history?

20. Believe in Bigfoot? ◯ Of course ◯ No way

21. Up to date on current news? ◯ Yes ◯ No

22. What's not fair? _____

23. ◯ Waffle cone ◯ Sugar cone ◯ Cup?

24. Favorite costume you've ever worn? _____

25. Which is worse? No ◯ TV ◯ Music

26. Best fairy tale? _____

27. ◯ Small purse ◯ Giant bag?

28. Ever have an imaginary friend? ◯ No ◯ Yes, _____

29. Can different foods touch on your plate? ◯ Yes ◯ No

30. Favorite pair of shoes? _____

{ Name given at birth?

○ **Coffee**
○ **Tea?**

What do your friends call you? ▶

Favorite holiday and why? ✔

What do you do when you're mad?

Favorite actor?

○ Radio ○ iPod
○ Other?

Favorite actress?

Ever won anything?
○ **yes** ○ **no**
✔What?

Flower u love? _ _ _ _ _ _ _ _ _ _ _

Oldest living relative? _ _ _ _ _ _ _ _ _

Most annoying bug? _ _ _ _ _ _ _ _ _ _

Best kind of music? _ _ _ _ _ _ _ _ _ _

○ 🐕 ○ 🐈
person?

What do you do on rainy days?

Ever been in love?
○ yes ○ no

○ **Tanning oil**
○ **Sunscreen?**

Nails:
○ Painted
○ Chipped
○ Fake
○ Bitten?

Wear painful shoes just because they're cute?
○ yes
○ no

Have a secret you've never told?
○ yes ○ no

Fave thing to nosh on? _ _ _ _ _ _ _ _ _ _ _ _ _ _ _ _ _ _

Did you ever believe in the Tooth Fairy?

○ yes ○ nah

Your absolute favorite article of clothing?

○ Spender ○ Saver?

What superpower would you love to have?

Cosmetic you can't live without?

○ Butterflies
○ Dragonflies?

Would you try?
○ **Skydiving**
○ **Rappelling**
○ **Scuba Diving**

○ Organic
○ Junk food?

Who do you wish you could meet? 👉

Best beverage?

Cereal you love?

Who should play you in a movie version of your life?
_ _

If you were an animal what would you be?
_ _

Best teacher you've ever had? _ _ _ _ _ _ _ _ _ _

Favorite school subject? _ _ _ _ _ _ _ _ _ _ _ _

● Fro yo
● Ice cream?

● Mall
● Outlet?

● Chips
● Fries?

● Fearless
● Fearful?

BEST FRIEND
SINCE KINDERGARTEN

1. Name? _____

2. Where were you born? _____

3. Favorite picture book? _____

4. ◯ Hot dog   ◯ Hamburger?

5. Invention you would love? _____

6. Friend you've had the longest? _____

7. ◯ White   ◯ Wheat?

8. Best fashion era?   ◯ 60s ◯ 70s ◯ 80s ◯ 90s ◯ Now

9. How many hours per day online? _____

10. How many hours per day texting? _____

11. What's scarier?   ◯ Snake   ◯ Shark

12. What do you always say "no" to? _____

13. Favorite food comes from which country? _____

14. Try to run away from home when you were little?   ◯ Yes ◯ No

15. What are you not good at? _____

16. Something you would like to try? _____

17. ⭘ Chocolate   ⭘ Soy   ⭘ Almond milk?

18. Friend who lives the farthest from you? _____

19. Where does #18 friend live? _____

20. Which could you give up? ⭘ Email   ⭘ Cell phone

21. ⭘ Flip-flops   ⭘ Strappy sandals?

22. Favorite season? _____ Why? _____

23. Read the ending before finishing a book? ⭘ Yes   ⭘ No

24. Who would you switch places with for one day? _____

25. ⭘ Island cabana   ⭘ European castle   ⭘ Safari tent   ⭘ Ski lodge?

26. What scared you as a little kid? _____

27. Favorite number? _____ Why? _____

28. ⭘ Right-handed   ⭘ Left-handed   ⭘ Ambidextrous?

29. Color your toes are painted? _____

30. Ever needed stitches? ⭘ No   ⭘ Yes, for _____

I always find animals in the clouds

1. Name? _____

2. Birthday? _____

3. Something you can't stand the smell of? _____

4. Look for shapes in the clouds? ◯ Yes ◯ No

5. Coolest thing you learned this week? _____

6. What are you good at? _____

7. ◯ Great vision ◯ Glasses ◯ Contacts?

8. Favorite take-out food? _____

9. Something you can't wait to do? _____

10. ◯ Salty ◯ Sweet?

11. Swallow anything by accident as a kid? ◯ No ◯ Yes, _____

12. Favorite accessory? _____

13. ◯ Lone Ranger ◯ Team Player?

14. ◯ Bikini ◯ One-piece?

15. Ever been snowed in? ◯ No ◯ Yes

I dream of flying to exotic lands

16. Take pictures with ◯ camera ◯ phone?

17. Something you like to listen to? _____

18. ◯ Tap ◯ Bottled ◯ Sparkling water?

19. What was your fave thing on the playground? _____

20. What would you love to see? _____

21. Favorite hot beverage? _____

22. Habit you wish you could change? _____

23. Are you a sore loser? ◯ Yes ◯ No

24. Yummiest ice cream flavor? _____

25. ◯ Pilot ◯ Navigator?

26. Who influences you the most? _____

27. Have you ever re-gifted? ◯ No ◯ Yes, _____

28. ◯ Toilet-papered ◯ Toilet-paperer?

29. What do you daydream about? _____

30. ◯ Small talk ◯ Deep conversation?

IF YOU LOVE THIS BOOK, CHECK OUT THESE OTHER COKE OR PEPSI? BOOKS!